I0166037

Anonymous

Select Psalms and hymns

For the use of the Parish Church of Cardington in the County of Bedford

Anonymous

Select Psalms and hymns
For the use of the Parish Church of Cardington in the County of Bedford

ISBN/EAN: 9783337273385

Printed in Europe, USA, Canada, Australia, Japan

Cover: Foto ©Lupo / pixelio.de

More available books at **www.hansebooks.com**

SELECT PSALMS,

CHRISTMAS HYMNS,

AND OTHER

Devotional and Sentimental Pieces,

BY WILLIAM CHRISTIE.

Author of JESUS THE MESSIAH, &c. A Sacred Poem in seven Cantos, and other publications in Prose and Verse.

While I live, I will praise the LORD : *I will sing praises unto my* GOD, *while I have any being.*

When the fulness of the time was come, GOD *sent forth his Son made of a woman.*

The Memory of the Just is blest.

PHILADELPHIA:

Printed by M'Carty & Davis, Printers and Booksellers, No. 204, Market Street.

....

1821.

EASTERN DISTRICT OF PENNSYLVANIA, to wit:

Be it remembered, That on the sixth day of July, in the forty-sixth year of the Independence of the United States of America, ‡ L. S. ‡ A. D. 1821, William Christie, of the said district, hath deposited in this office, the title of a book the right whereof he claims as Author, in the words following, to wit:

" Select Psalms, Christmas Hymns, and other Devotional and Senti-
" mental Pieces, by William Christie. Author of Jesus the Messiah,
" &c. A Sacred Poem in seven Cantos, and other publications in
" Prose and Verse. While I live I will praise the Lord: I will sing
" praises unto my God; while I have any being. When the fulness of
" the time was come, God sent forth his Son made of a woman. The
" memory of the just is blest.

In conformity to the act of the Congress of the United States, intituled, " An Act for the encouragement of learning, by securing the copies of maps, charts, and books, to the authors and proprietors of such copies, during the times therein mentioned." And also to the act, entitled, " An Act supplementary to an act, entitled, 'An Act for the encouragement of learning, by securing the copies of maps, charts and books to the authors and proprietors of such copies, during the times therein mentioned,' and extending the benefits thereof to the arts of designing, engraving, and etching historical and other prints."

D. CALDWELL,
Clerk of the Eastern District of Pennsylvania.

PREFACE.

THE Collection of Sacred Odes or Hymns styled *Psalms* has been deservedly esteemed by devout and serious minds in all ages, since their first appearance in Hebrew. The ancient Israelites had a national music of their own. We find prefixed to several Psalms the following words : "To the chief Musician." At this distance of time we cannot precisely conceive what effect these Psalms must have had upon the minds of the hearers when sung in the original, national language by able performers, and accompanied with every variety of instrumental music. If they appear to us so beautiful in a literal prose translation, or when turned into verse by a good poet, and sung in our churches, either, vocally, or joined with the solemn sound of the organ ; how astonishing, how transporting must their effect have been upon the natives of Judea, when chanted or sung in the manner before described.

The Hebrew Bards, excel all other ancient poets, in dignity of subject, sublimity united with simplicity of expression, true pathos, and unaffected elegance. In a word, no man of real taste, and intelligence, can read these animated compositions, without discovering at once, that the Nation from which they came must have had an immediate communication with the Deity, that no other nation was favoured with, either before or after. In the Psalms we find express mention made of Moses and his institutions, the plagues inflicted upon Egypt, the passage of the Red Sea, the drowning of impious Pharoah and his host, the wonders performed in the wilderness, the rolling back the river Jordan, the triumphant entrance of the Israelites into the land of Canaan, their taking possession of it, with every other important fact in the early part of the Jewish history.

Nor is this all, I am convinced from a perusal of these Psalms, that the ancient Jews had a comfortable expectation and belief of a future state of rewards and punishments : and this opinion is confirmed by passages in the Prophets, in the New Testament, and in the Apocryphal writers. I conceive also that the ancient Patriarchs entertained this belief, that it existed among good men, before the flood, and was probably revealed by GOD to Adam himself, after the fall. I am well apprized, that this statement has been denied by some very learned and ingenious

men ; no doubt from good motives. To argue the matter
would lead me too far : I can do no more, at present, but declare my opinion.

Farther, I apprehend, that there are in these Psalms express
predictions of *Jesus the Messiah*, and the glories of his kingdom, in the latter days.   I apprehend this assertion is fully
confirmed by the words of our LORD himself in a passage re-
ferred to below.*

The absolute denial of the doctrine of atonement in the
title I have prefixed to Psalm xxxii. may appear wonderful
to some, not acquainted with the discussions that this doctrine has undergone.   I am satisfied myself; though I may
not be able to satisfy others.   The doctrine of atonement
rests chiefly upon some figurative passages in the New Testament, and in Isaiah ; but is inconsistent with the general
tenor of both Testaments, is expressly contradicted in the
Psalms, by the Prophets, and by our LORD himself, the *Apostle
and High Priest of our Profession*.   It is absolutely inconsistent with the Doctrine of *Free Grace*, as stated by the Apostle
Paul, and when joined with another doctrine nearly allied to
it, it is justification *by works* in the strongest terms. Perhaps,
some pious, worthy persons, in the sincerity of their hearts may
say.   " How can JESUS be called a Saviour, if he did not die
for us, and make atonement for our sins." I answer, JESUS
CHRIST, certainly died for you, and all mankind ; that is, he
would not have died, if you and others had not sinned : but
he did not die to make an atonement for your sins, if you
mean by the word *atonement*, to make satisfaction to GOD for
them.   For GOD *is love*, and requires no other satisfaction but
sincere repentance, confession, and reformation, even that, *godly sorrow which worketh repentance not to be repented of.*
Farther, JESUS CHRIST our blessed LORD, is a *Saviour* in an
exalted sense, without making atonement, that is, satisfaction
to GOD,

1. By declaring the will of GOD more fully than any other
Prophet had done before him, and by appointing his apostles
to *teach*, (or proselyte) *all nations ;* breaking down the parti-
tion-wall between Jews and Gentiles, and uniting all mankind
in the common worship of JEHOVAH ; *his Father, and our Father, his God, and our God.*

2. By setting the doctrine of immortality, or a *Resurrection
from the dead* in a clearer light than ever it had been exhibited before ; by his discourses on the subject, and above all by
his public Crucifixion, and well attested Resurrection.   In
this and other similar senses he may be said to *die for our sins,
and to rise again for our Justification,* " GOD forbid.! that I
" should glory save in the *cross* of our LORD JESUS CHRIST."

* Luke xxiv. 44.

3. Because, *as by* MAN *came death, so by* MAN *came also the resurrection of the dead: for as in Adam all die, even so in Christ shall all be made alive.*   Had not GOD been, or acted *in* or *by* CHRIST, *reconciling the world unto himself,* all mankind had remained under the sentence of death for ever, without the possibility of a revival.   In this sense, particularly, CRHIST *is the Resurrection and the life.*   But observe very carefully, that in this and other passages of the New Testament, CHRIST is never said to reconcile GOD to men, but to reconcile men to GOD.   For GOD requires no reconciliation, he was always reconciled to his creatures, calling upon them, entreating them, saying, " turn ye, turn ye, from your evil ways ; for why will ye die, O house of Israel !"   It is only men that need to be reconciled to GOD, to be cured of all their evil passions, to repent and amend ; and this, CHRIST will do abundantly, if men will listen to his instructions.

Much more might be said, even in a brief way, on this highly important subject ; and other senses in which JESUS is a Saviour, a Redeemer or deliverer, might be brought forward, particularly, in his present state of exaltation ; by a critical investigation and explanation of some high epithets applied to him in the Revelation.   But this I have already done in former publications ; and none of these epithets imply more than what a glorified MAN, with a plenitude of inspiration and divine powers may be thought capable of performing. But I return, from this digression to my proper subject.

Soon after the Reformation *Buchanan* published an elegant version of the Psalms, in every variety of Latin measure, which was greatly admired by the learned in Europe, particularly by the first *Scahger.*   Long after, *Johnston,* another Scotsman, favoured the admirers of Latin poetry with a new translation in Hexameter verse.   Some think there is more of the elegant simplicity of the original preserved in this version than the former.

I have had in my possession, in former days, two French versions of the Psalms, composed by Protestants in that country.   The earliest of these, being in old French, I paid little attention to: the latest, I thought elegant at the time ; but could not at present repeat a single stanza.   *Jean Baptiste Rousseau,* a Catholic, has rendered a few Psalms in French verse with a great deal of spirit ; but many years have elapsed since I perused them.

The oldest English version of the Psalms that I am acquainted with is that of *Sternhold and Hopkins,* still in use, I believe, in the church of England, though that of Tate and Brady has deservedly superseded it in many places.   This version is, in general, miserably harsh and unpoetical.   Notwithstanding, there are two stanzas in Psalm xviii, which

have been greatly admired, particularly by Dr. Beattie, and
with the alteration of one word would make a lofty sense, indeed!

Having mentioned the name of Dr. *Beattie*, I will give an
extract from a small Tract, of his " on the Improvement of
" Psalmody, in Scotland, in a Letter to the Rev. Hugh Blair,
" D. D. &c. 1778." The name of Dr. Beattie does not stand
in the Title-page ; but I know *certainly* that he was the author.
I knew Dr. Beattie well, his family and connections in Scotland, and could tell many anecdotes concerning him, not re-
corded by, and probably not known to Sir Wm. Forbes, his
Biographer.

Some part of this letter is employed in a critical disquisi-
tion respecting the merits of *Tate and Brady's* version, and
that in use, in the established churches in Scotland.   He gives
a decided preference to the latter, and thinks that with some
improvements it might be made the best of any.   I agree with
him in the main ; though I think he rather bears too hard on
Tate and Brady's version. He praises exceedingly King James's
version, and also a few Psalms that the great *Milton* translated.
But now for the quotation.

" I have seen five other translations of the psalms in verse;
" that were printed in England during the last century ; by
" Joshua Squire, Luke Milbourn, Daniel Burgess, George
" Wither, and Richard Goodridge ; but I did not find any
" thing in them worthy of further notice.   Two were publish-
" ed a few years ago, one by Mr. Smart, the other by Mr.
" Merrick. I have not seen these ; but, from what I know of the
" authors, I am satisfied that they well deserve the public atten-
" tion."

" The learned and ingenious Dr. Watts translated the psalms
" into verse ; adapting the sentiments to the language and doc-
" trines of the New Testament.   His imagination as a poet,
" was not brilliant; and his numbers are rather smooth than
" harmonious ; but his verse is easy, and his expression simple.
" I have great respect for the memory of that good man and
" excellent writer, as well as for the judgment of many of those
" who approve his translation.   But I freely own, that it is not
" to my taste, though I cannot here give my reasons.   If we
" mean to use the psalms of David in our worship, I humbly
" think, that we should take them as they are ; without sup-
" posing, either that they are not so good as they ought to be,
" or that it is in our power to make them better. I allow indeed,
" that new-testament-hymns have at least an equal claim to our
" veneration, but I would not make a parody of the Scripture,
" by expressing the sentiments of the one Testament in the
" words of the other.   However I will not enter into the con-
" troversy, which would lead me too far from my present

" purpose. I shall only remark, that some of Dr. Watts' psalms
" are both elegant and *literal*, and may be of great use to the
" person who undertakes to execute the following plan."

I make no remarks upon what Dr. Beattie says in general respecting Watts' Psalms.   But there is one assertion that I cannot let pass.   " His imagination as a poet was not brilliant."
I am conscious that I was born a poet* as well as Dr. Beattie,
and may therefore give my opinion concerning a matter of taste.
Dr. Watts when he composed his Psalms and Hymns levelled
his superior genius to the conceptions and feelings of those for
whose benefit he wrote ; but in his Lyric poems, he gives full
scope to his powers as a poet.

> " Sov'reign of sacred verse, accept the lays,
> " Of a young bard that dares attempt thy praise,
> " A muse the meanest of the vocal throng,
> " New to the bays, nor equal to the song.
> " Fir'd with the growing glories of thy name,
> " Joins all her pow'rs to celebrate thy fame."

> " And *Addison* thy tuneful song approves."

I have read these lines in a British Edition of Watts' Lyric
poems, at least fifty years ago, and have reason to believe, that
they came from the pen of Dr. *Young*.   Dr. *Johnson* in his
lives of the English Poets, speaking of Watts' sacred poetry
says, " he has done better than others, what nobody has done
well."   A great compliment from a high-churchman to a dis-
senting Minister. Dr. Johnson, with amiable candour, bestows
other encomiums on Watts, which I must omit.

I come now to speak of what I have endeavoured to perform
myself.   In moral and penitential Psalms I kept as close as I
could to the sense and even the words of the Psalmist.   In
Psalms that may be called descriptive or philosophical, I have
indulged myself in a greater latitude.   The only moral psalm,
that I have translated with much freedom is the *first*.   What I
have done there may be rather called a Paraphrase than a Version.

These pieces were composed in Spring 1818, in the space
of *three weeks*.   During this time, I was almost in a state
of abstraction from mortality, only intent upon the great
work I had in hand.   I never felt the *vis poetica* in so
high a degree in my life : nor did it ever continue with me, in
force, for so long a period.   At the close, however, I became
exhausted, and fell deplorably low.

> ———— " What are we ?
> " How unequal ! now we soar,
> " And now we sink.   To be the same transcends
> " Our present prowess."

> " Our utmost strength, when down, to rise again,
> " And not to yield, tho' beaten, all our praise."

* Poeta nascitur, non fit.—Hor.

Three years have elapsed since these versions were finished, yet I have never been able to add any thing to them, that deserves to be named : and I presume, I shall never be able to tune the harp of *Moses*, of *David*, of *Asaph*, successfully again. Such as they are, I recommend them to the blessing of GOD, and send them abroad into the world. The other poems I have published will speak for themselves. I have been obliged to suppress for want of room, and to prevent too great expence, some pieces that I intended to have published. With every good wish for *all that name the name of* CHRIST, I finish this publication.

Philadelphia,   **WILLIAM CHRISTIE.**
July 5th, 1821.

PSALMS, CHRISTMAS HYMNS,

AND OTHER

Devotional and Sentimental Pieces.

Psalm I.

The happiness of the Good Man, contrasted with the misery and dreadful end of Sinners.

1 What blessedness attends the man,
　Whose wise and elevated plan
　　Is measured by the law divine;
　Who shuns deceitful paths and vain,
　Disclaims the wicked and profane,
　　But bends to truth and virtue's shrine.

2 His holy labours cheer the day
　And make the evening season gay,
　　A source of rational delight;
　Keep passion under strict controul,
　Improve and sanctify the soul,
　　With knowledge pure and heav'nly light.

3 Like a well-grown and stately tree,
　His mind is still erect and free,
　　Enrich'd with pious blossoms fair;
　Refresh'd with moisture at the root,
　The branches full of vigour shoot,
　　And estimable produce bear.

B

4 His prosperous course he still pursues,
Fill'd with delightful hopes and views,
  With resignation and content:
While Vice its votaries misleads,
And hurries on in evil deeds,
  Till life in infamy is spent.

5 No solid bliss for such remain,
Their hopes equivocal and vain,
  Shall fly like chaff by whirlwinds driven,
And leave them helpless, wretched, poor,
Torn from their wealth and ill-earn'd store,
  Strangers to happiness and heaven.

ɔ For guilt in Judgment shall not stand,
Nor sinners join the righteous band,
  But must be sever'd and depart:
For GOD approves the pure and just,
Will raise, and bless them, from the dust,
  While sinners meet their due desert.

Psalm VIII.

The Sovereignty and Infinite Benevolence of GOD; *and
his goodness to Man in granting him Dominion over
the Creatures.*

JEHOVAH! Architect divine,
Both heaven and earth, and all are thine,
The glory of thy peerless name
Extends throughout the starry frame,
And fills the whole creation bright
With admiration and delight.

Even babes and sucklings learn thy ways,
And magnify thy name with praise,
And by thy aid exert a strength
Which bears down every foe at length.

When I lift up my wond'ring eyes,
And view the glories of the skies,

The moon and stars in order just,
And view myself—poor breathing dust!
With deep prostration down I fall,
Before thy face—the LORD of all :
Compell'd to say—LORD, What is man?
Whose strength is weakness—age a span,
That thou the great SUPREME should'st deign,
To notice even a thing so vain.
Created by thy power and might,
A little less than angels bright,
With dignity and glory grac'd, ·
And in a sovereign province plac'd ;
Thy mercies which no limits know,
Have made him Lord of all below,
Subjected to his rule and sway,
The creatures of earth, air and sea.
O LORD ! the glories of thy name
Resound throughout creation's frame.

Psalm xv.

Virtuous Integrity, or the moral picture of an Upright Man.

LORD ! in thy temple who shall dwell?
And occupy thy holy hill?
The Man who upright paths pursues,
And RIGHT respects in all he does :
Who never will from Truth depart,
Assume the base dissembler's part,
But speak the language of his heart.
He will not do his neighbour wrong,
Nor vilify him with his tongue ;
Meanly applaud before his face,
But absent, censure with ill-grace.
Detraction's path he hates to tread,
And bad reports forbears to spread ;
Vice he contemns, though rais'd on high,
But honours Godly Poverty.

His sacred Oath or promise pure,
Though hurtful to himself is sure;
Of Usury he scorns the plan,
Is just and kind to every man.
For no bribe or emolument,
He will betray the innocent.
    The Man who keeps this steady course,
Undeviating to the worse;
By God accepted and approv'd
Shall never from his place be mov'd.

Psalm XIX.

*GOD manifested by the magnificence of the works of
Nature, and by the Revelation of his Will; or Reason
and Scripture united.*

1 Through the immensity of space,
    Where starry orbs perform their rounds
With constant and unwearied pace ;—
    The great CREATOR's name resounds :
Day speaks to day th' exalted theme,
And Night to night repeats the same.

2 No vocal language they possess,
    Yet reason in persuasive strain,
Each region hears their grand address,
    And every different class of men :
From age to age they roll and shine,
.And still proclaim the power divine.

3 The Sun in flaming radiance drest,
    Like a young Bridegroom fresh and gay,
Starts from his quarters in the east
    To cheer and animate the day :
Dispensing with unceasing strife,*
Light, heat, and vegetable life.

* The word *strife* is here used in a sense similar to *exertion* or *influence*.

4 The silver Moon affords her light,
  And sheds a mitigated ray,
To cheer the darkness of the night,
  Sent to supply the place of day :
Presents an aspect clear, serene,
While brilliant Stars complete the scene.

5 From the bright view of Nature's frame,
  We turn to view the law divine,
That law, which with well-founded claim,
  Is *perfect* styl'd, and all benign :
Converts the soul from earth to heaven,
In mercy great to mankind given.

6 This heavenly testimony prize,
  In worth, indeed, above all rate,
It makes the simple-minded wise,
  And guides them to a happy state :
The Statutes of the LORD are right,
Without ambiguous meaning, bright.

7 His precepts clear, distinct and pure,
  Enlighten all attending eyes,
Instruct the rich, exalt the poor,
  The Fear divine leads to the skies :
Founded in equity and truth,
Comfort of age, and guard of youth.

8 Compar'd with these, Wealth has no price,
  Golconda's diamonds, Peru's gold,
Splendid possessions, garments nice,
  Scarce merit to be nam'd or told :
Sweeter than honey, virgin pure,
Who has them never can be poor.

9 Moreover they with faithful care,
  Give warning to our heedless course,
Avoiding every hurtful snare,
  To choose the better, shun the worse :
Rewards exuberant attend
All those who keep them to the end.

10 Who can his errors comprehend,
        From secret guilt LORD cleanse my soul,
    And from presumptuous sins restrain'd
        May I be by thy kind controul :
    That innocent I still may be,
    Upright, from great transgression free.

11 These words that from my mouth proceed,
        These meditations of my heart
    Accept O LORD, for thou, indeed,
        My Strength and my Redeemer art :
    Through Life, I, in thy love will trust,
    In Death, to raise me from the dust,—
    To bless thy name to see thy face,
    And evermore adore thy grace.

Psalm XXIII.

*The pastoral care of God over his Servants, in Life, in
Death, and for ever.*

    JEHOVAH is my Shepherd kind,
    I shall not want, but always find
    Constant supplies of daily food,
    With every other needful good.
    Under his conduct I repose
    In verdure where mild water flows ;
    My soul ennobled by his grace,
    He leads in paths of righteousness ;
    And for his own name's sake divine,
    Vouchsafes on me a look benign.

    Yea, though I walk with panting breath
    Through the dark vale and shade of death,
    My heart assur'd shall fear no ill,
    For thou, my GOD, art with me still,
    Thy rod and staff shall there attend
    To help me near my journey's end.

My Table thou hast made to stand
In presence of a hostile band :
My head's perfum'd with oil in store,
And my replenish'd cup runs o'er.

Goodness and mercy all my days
Shall follow me, and cheer my ways ;
And in thy house O LORD I'll dwell
For ever, and thy goodness tell.

Psalm xxiv.

*GOD the sole Creator and Proprietor of the World.
Integrity exhibited and recommended.   An allusion
to the triumphal procession under the conduct of David,
when the* ARK OF GOD *was replaced in the Tabernacle.*

The *Earth* and all that it contains
Is great JEHOVAH's just domains :
The *World* and all that there reside;
His power produc'd, his counsels guide,
Upon the seas and rolling flood
He fix'd it, and pronounc'd it *good.*

Who shall ascend the sacred hill,
And in GOD's house a station fill,—
The Man whose hands no stains defile,
Whose heart is pure and free from guile ;
Whose humble, uncorrupted soul,
No passions vain, lift up, controul ;
Whose stern, confirm'd, integrity
Hath never sworn deceitfully.

This is the just, the pious race
Who seek the GOD of Jacob's face.

Ye gates lift up your shining head,
Ye everlasting doors be spread ;
Admit the KING OF GLORY great,
With his attending *Train* in state !

Who is this *King of Glory* bright?
JEHOVAH! infinite in might:
The single, self-sufficient, LORD!
Who rules, and conquers by a *Word!**

Psalm XXXII.

*The inexpressible Happiness of the Man, who has expiat-
ed, and atoned for, his Sins, by sincere Repentance and
Amendment. The only atonement that* GOD *desires
or that* Man *can give.*

" For thou desirest not Sacrifice, else would I give
" it thee : thou delightest not in burnt offering. The
" Sacrifices of GOD are a broken spirit : a broken and
" a contrite heart, O GOD, thou wilt not despise."
David? Psalm li. 16, 17.

O State of bliss and joy within,
To feel a sense of pardon'd Sin !
To know the LORD of Earth and Heaven
Hath all our numerous sins forgiven !
While on my mind the burden lay,
My Conscience smarted night and day :
Reflection no relief could bring,
But added sharpness to the sting.

My prayer I to the LORD address'd,
And eas'd the troubles of my breast ;
Confessing with a contrite heart
My sins, without reserve, or art.

The LORD whose mercies never cease,
Vouchsaf'd to me his heavenly grace ;
Spoke peace to my afflicted mind,
With love transcendent, free, and kind.

The Godly man for sin forgiven,
Will still renew his suit to heaven :

* The intelligent, inquiring Reader, is here recommended to the perusal
of a passage in " Discourses on the Divine Unity." VIII. page 127, 1st Edition, Montrose, 1784.

And with acceptance he will pray,
And mercy find of GOD alway,

When waters great shall overflow,
Unhurt by them, he'll come and go :
For GOD will be his sure retreat,
His shield from troubles small or great :
When adverse events round him throng,
Deliv'rance still shall be his song.

GOD will instruct, and teach the way,
And guard him, that he shall not stray,
Will view him with his watchful eye,
And listen to his earnest cry.

Wisdom befits the thinking mind,
Superior to the brutal kind,
Whose savage force must be restrain'd
And from committing mischief, chain'd.

Sorrow shall fill the wicked's cup,
While righteous men rejoice in hope ;
And firmly trusting in the LORD,
Find ease and comfort in his *Word.*

Let righteous men rejoice in GOD,
And testify their joy abroad;
A cheerful shout becomes the part
Of all who are upright in heart.

Psalm XXXIII.

The Righteous called upon to rejoice in GOD, *and to ce-*
lebrate his Name. The glory of the CREATOR *display-*
ed in the works of Creation and Providence.

1 Ye righteous in the LORD rejoice,
    For cheerful praise becomes th' upright;
To him lift up your grateful voice,
    Let sacred strains be your delight :
Compose a new and lofty song ;
With accents loud the notes prolong.

C

2 God's word is purity and Right,
  And all his works perform'd in truth :
 The Earth is full of beauties bright,
  And goodness in perpetual growth :
No where we turn our wond'ring eyes,
But objects of fresh grace arise.

3 The powerful *fiat* of the Lord,
  Call'd forth the firmament on high,
 With orbs innumerable stor'd,
  Which fill and ornament the sky :
Establish'd by his breath divine,
With infinitely wise design.

4 The wat'ry element he guides,
  And lays together as an heap,
 In store-house strong it still abides,
  And must its place and station keep :
Nor can it overflow or pass,
Beyond the fix'd appointed place.

5 Can the astonish'd Earth forbear,
  With such a scene before it spread,
 The Lord to magnify and fear,
  And to displease him be afraid :
O let its nations stand in awe,
Revere his name, obey his law !

6 When God in majesty direct,
  Resolv'd the starry worlds to frame ;
 His end and purpose to effect,
  Requir'd him but the thing to name :
He spake,—and all his will took place,
Commanded,—Nature rose in grace.

7 The Heathen tribes consult in vain,
  Jehovah brings their schemes to nought ;
 The People's plans he doth restrain,
  And disappoints each sinful thought :
But his most perfect counsels, sure,
Through generations all endure.

8 The Nation how supremely blest,
  Whose God acknowledg'd is the Lord;
That nation shall securely rest
  As *his*, if they obey his word:
No hostile force shall them assail,
Or daring, shall completely fail.

9 The Lord Omnipotent looks down
  From heaven, upon our earthly race,
The poor, and he who wears a crown,
  He views with equal eye and grace:
Alike he frames their various minds,
Reviews their works and their designs.

10 A host of warriors shall not save
  A King from death or shameful flight;
The strong shall fill an early grave,
  Who trusted in his skill and might:
A courser swift no safety bring,
But found a vain defenceless thing.

11 The Lord with pitying eye, benign,
  Will view all those who fear his name,
Trust in his mercy, and resign
  Themselves, and all they have to him:
He will deliver them from death,
In famine still preserve their breath.

12 Our souls with fervour wait the Lord,
  He is our shield, our hope, our fame;
In him we'll joy with sweet accord,
  Still trusting in his holy name:
Thy mercy Lord to us extend,
Hoping in thee till life shall end.

Psalm xxxiv.

The Care and Compassion of God *for good Men: their
Prayers heard and accepted by him.*

At all times, I will bless the Lord,
His Love continually record :
My soul shall make her boast in God,
And signify the theme abroad;
The humble, when they hear, shall joy,
And join me in the sweet employ.

O magnify the Lord with me,
Exalt his Name in accents free ;
I sought the Lord, he heard my prayers,
And still'd all my uneasy fears.

They look'd on him and were reliev'd,
Nor were their hearts and faces griev'd
The poor man cry'd, the Lord did hear,
And caus'd his troubles disappear.

The Angel of the Lord surrounds
His Servants, and their foes confounds.
See, taste, the goodness of the Lord,
How blest the man who trusts his word!

O ye his Saints still fear his Name,
And he'll secure from want and shame :
The young rapacious Lions may
Feel hungry for the want of prey ;
But those who truly seek the Lord,
To them he'll every good afford.

Come children, hearken to my word,
I'll teach you how to fear the Lord.
The Man whose wishes and desire
To life and happy days aspire,
Must keep his tongue from every ill,
And guard his lips from speaking guile ;
From every evil deed depart,
Seek peace, do good, with all his heart.

God views with a propitious eye
The righteous, and will hear their cry;
But with displeasure shews his face
Against the undeserving race
Of Sinners, and will certanly
Cut off their noxious memory.

The Righteous unto God *most high*
Address their prayers and humble cry :
The Lord with approbation hears,
Dispels their troubles and their fears.

The Lord is ready to impart
Safety to men of contrite heart.
Afflictions on the righteous press,
But God relieves them in distress :
Their bones unbroken shall remain
For useful service, void of pain.

Evil shall slay the wicked all,
And desolation on them fall :
But God his Servants will redeem,
And none shall sink, who trust in him.

Psalm XXXVII.

Good Men admonished against distrust of Divine Provi-
dence, Envy and Impatience. The excellence aud hap-
piness of the Righteous; the deformity and baseness
of the Wicked, beautifully contrasted.

Let not thy anxious mind repine
For each iniquitous design,
By evil-minded men conceiv'd,
And oft successfully atchiev'd :
For short shall be their prosperous state,
Calamitous their final fate.
Soon shall they be cut down like grass,
And wither'd as the green herb pass.

Do good, and in the LORD confide,
And thou shalt in the land abide,
Thy food and raiment be supply'd,
And thy just wishes gratify'd.

Let GOD be thy supreme delight,
Implore his grace and heavenly light:
To gain his favour still aspire,
And he will grant thy just desire.

Commit unto the LORD thy way,
Trust in him, strict obedience pay;
And he thy honest plans will bless,
And give thy lawful aims success;
Thy righteousness he shall display,
And place thy worth in open day.

Rest in the LORD, and wait his will,
In patience still possess your soul,
Let no invidious thought take place,
Rankle thy heart, disturb thy peace;
Because a wicked man succeeds
And brings to pass his evil deeds.

From wrath and hostile passions cease,
Nor ill attempt in any case:
For evil doers strive in vain,
Their wicked works shall not remain:
To those upon the LORD that wait,
On earth he'll grant a happy state.

The wicked soon shall cease to be,
His very place thou shalt not see:
But meek men shall the earth enjoy
In peaceful plans themselves employ.

The wicked plot against the just,
And rage at those the LORD who trust;
The LORD on high shall him deride,
Confound his schemes abase his pride,
He sees the future day at hand
Prepar'd to crush at his command.

Sinners with hostile arms assail
The upright poor, but they shall fail;
Their sword shall pierce their bosoms all,
Their broken bows to pieces fall.

The righteous man with grateful heart
Receives what God is pleas'd t' impart:
His little stores in worth excel
The riches that with ill men dwell.
Their arms the wicked shall not hold,
But God the righteous will uphold.
God knows the days of the upright,
For ever lasts their portion bright:
They shall not blush when evils spread,
In famine God will grant them bread.

But wicked men shall fast decay;
The foes of God shall melt away;
Like fat all shall dissolve in smoke,
Who impiously the LORD provoke.

The wicked, with deceitful plan,
Borrows, but pays not back again:
The righteous in mercy lends,
And even gives to help his friends:
His blessing lasting good procures
On earth: His curse distress ensures.

A good man's steps, his conduct right,
Are order'd by the LORD of might:
For he delighteth in his way,
Upholds and cheers him all the day.
Though he should fall unguardedly,
Not utterly cast down he'll be:
The LORD his kind protector will
With friendly hand uphold him still.

I have been young, now old become,
The righteous without a home
I've never seen, nor yet his seed
Compell'd to beg their daily bread:
He's ever merciful, and lends,
His seed is blest, and will find friends.

Depart from evil, and pursue
All good, with steady steps and true,
And you for evermore shall dwell,
In peace, and love and mercy tell.

The LORD our Maker justice loves,
Leaves not his saints, but still approves ;
Keeps them for ever : but the seed
Of impious men shall not succeed.

The righteous in the land, as heirs
Shall dwell, and find it ever theirs :
True wisdom from their mouths proceed,
And judgment just in word and deed :
The law of GOD is in his heart,
None of his steps from it depart.

The wicked with a savage joy
Watcheth the righteous to destroy :
GOD will not leave him to his will,
Nor punish, but acquit him still.

Wait on the LORD, and keep his way,
And he shall thee exalt to stay ;
To flourish in the land, and see
The wicked torn from it, and thee.

The wicked in great pow'r I've seen,
Himself spread out like bay-tree green :
When lo, he pass'd, and was no more,
I sought in vain his place before.

Do thou with strict attention scan
The upright, godly, perfect man,
Whose pious labours never cease,
For certainly his end is peace.

But sad destruction shall befal
The group of foul transgressors all :
Dismal shall be the wicked's end,
Without a GOD, without a friend.

But men to righteousness inclin'd,
Salvation from the LORD shall find ;
In present trouble he's their strength,
And will relieve from all at length.
The LORD shall them assistance give,
And send deliv'rance while they live.
From wicked men shall them redeem,
And save them, as they trust in him.

Psalm L.

The Judgment of God. Hypocrisy censured and con-
demned.

The mighty GOD, th' eternal LORD hath spoke,
His long, misjudg'd, continued, silence broke,
And summon'd all who fill the Earth, to come
To hear a pleasing or an awful doom :
From where the Sun displays an early ray,
Even to the distant clime, where ends the day.

From Zion the Supreme, all-perfect Mind,
Adorn'd with matchless beauty, GOD hath shin'd.
Our GOD shall surely come, and shall no more
Keep a mysterious silence, as before ;
Torrents of scorching fire before him fly,
And storms impetuous rend th' ethereal sky :
On high, in glorious majesty array'd,
He calls to heaven and earth, and all he made,
To judge his people, who profess his Name,
He comes, and either will applaud or blame.
My Saints collect, and those about me spread,
Who by known rites a Covenant have made :
The heavens his righteous Judgment shall declare,
For GOD the sovereign Judge himself is there.

My chosen people, *Israel*, hear my voice,
And I will testify against thy choice ;
D

For God I am, thy God, for ever blest,
Confirm'd and ratify'd by every test :
For ritual service, I will not reprove,
When join'd with holy zeal and fervent love :
I'll take no bullock from thy fold or stall,
No goat to me in sacrifice shall fall :
For every beast I claim by right divine,
The cattle on a thousand hills are mine :
The fowls on distant mountains all are known,
The savage beasts of every field I own :
Could piercing hunger ever me assail,
This pressing want to thee I would not tell :
The world itself with its contents are mine,
All held by my prerogative divine :
Will ever I the flesh of bulls partake,
Or from the blood of goats refreshment take :
To God thy gratitude and thanks present,
And pay thy vows to the omnipotent :
Then in the dreary day when troubles press,
Call upon me, and I'll remove distress,
And thou adoring shall my goodness bless.

    But to the wicked, God shall surely say,
What right hast thou my statutes to display,
That thou should'st take my cov'nant in thy mouth,
Oppos'd to Virtue from thy early youth.
Instruction thou hast hated to obey,
And my blest words profanely cast away :
A Thief with approbation thou hast seen,
And with Adulterers partaker been :
Thy mouth to evil-speaking thou hast given,
And fram'd deceit before all-seeing heaven :
From sordid views thy brother thou hast blam'd,
With slanders vile thy mother's son defam'd :
These deeds atrocious have thy life disgrac'd,
Whilst I kept silence, nor these wrongs redress'd :
Thy mind presumptuous, blinded and impure,
Conceiv'd that I such evils would endure :
But I will now reprove thee, and display
Thy vicious practices in open day.

Consider this, ye that forget the LORD,
When I chastise you, none can help afford.
The Man whose sacrifice is humble praise,
I hold to glorify my Name always :
And who uprightly speaks and acts below,
To him I'll my complete Salvation show.

Psalm xc.

The Eternity, Perfection, and infinite power of GOD, *compared with the frailty, Sinfulness and short duration of Man. Supplications for comfort and assistance in old age.*

1 Thou hast through every age and scene,
A Refuge to thy People been ;
Most gracious LORD of earth and heaven,
Eternal praise to thee be given.

2 Before the mountains were brought forth,
Before thy power had form'd the earth,
Of Deity supreme possess'd,
Thou wast from everlasting bless'd.

3 To sinful Man, prone to decay,
With awful justice, thou dost say,
From dust I rear'd your earthly frame,
Return to dust from whence ye came.

4 A thousand long successive years,
To thee, as yesterday appears :
Or like a transient watch at night,
Which vanishes at morning light.

5 Our race from the sweet face of day,
As floods thou carriest away :
Awhile we walk on earth or creep,
And then dissolve in dust, and sleep.

6 Or like the short liv'd morning grass,
Which evening withers, so we pass :
For we before thine anger fall,
And thy just wrath consumes us all.

7 Our Sins appear before thy sight,
Our secret faults in open light :
Our days from thy displeasure fail,
Our fleeting years pass like a tale.

8 Our term of life is seventy years :
How short, when past, this term appears :
If some see fourscore years, or more,
Weakness and pain afflict them sore ;
And soon the thread of life is broke,
And they are borne away like smoke.

9 Thine anger's power, who knows, can bear,
Thy wrath's according to thy fear :
So teach us Lord to count our days,
That we may walk in wisdom's ways.

10 Return, O Lord, without delay,
Thy Servants help who humbly pray :
Diffuse thy mercy's early rays,
To cheer our yet remaining days.

11 O grant us days and years serene,
For those in which we've evil seen :
Afflictive trials we have borne,
Let joy and comfort now return.

12 Thy saving work, let it appear,
To us thy willing Servants here :
Thy glory to our children show ;
O may they walk with God below.

13 Thy grace and beauty, Lord, divine,
May they upon us ever shine :
Our labours condescend to bless,
Confirm'd in truth and righteousness.

Psalm CIII.

The Goodness and Impartial Justice of GOD *celebrated.*
His Compassion and Tender Mercy to his Children re-
corded. All Beings in heaven and earth called upon to
praise him.

1 With grateful feelings in full power,
    The LORD THY MAKER call to mind;
  Whose Love and Mercy, every hour,
    Prove him benevolent and kind.

2 With constant, unremitting zeal,
    GOD's holy name for ever bless;
  Whose bounty, sovereign power to heal,
    Enlivened health and eas'd distress.

3 Whose grace spontaneous, unconfin'd,
    Pronounces all thy sins forgiven;
  Heals thee in body and in mind,
    And fills thee with the hope of heaven.

4 Wasted with sickness, try'd with pain,
    Brought to the borders of the grave;
  To help thee he did not refrain,
    But stretch'd his gracious hand to save.

5 His loving-kindness still survives,
    His tender mercies yet are shown,
  With food he cherishes our lives,
    My powers renew'd his goodness own.

6 An equal Judgment GOD displays,
    Sends timely aid to those oppress'd;
  To *Moses* he made known his ways,
    And gave his chosen *Israel* rest.

7 GOD's mercy is of large extent,
    His love and favour know no bound;
  To anger slow and punishment,
    Prone to forgive, averse to wound.

8 Eternally he will not chide,
  Nor keep his wrath for evermore :
  Mercy with him shall still abide,
  And loving-kindness in full store.

9 As heaven in majestic height,
  Exceeds the low terrestrial frame ;
  So great appears his mercy bright,
  To those who love and fear his name.

10 Far as the eastern region spreads
   In distance from the western shore,
   His love removes from guilty heads,
   Those sad transgressions they deplore.

11 As a fond Father's care and love,
   With pity views his infant race,
   Like pity shews the LORD above,
   To all who fear him, trust his grace.

12 For well he knows our earthly frame,
   Our frail original from dust :
   A transient blast impairs the same,
   It perishes before the gust.

13 A flow'r, a creature of a day
   Which flutters on our earthly scene,
   Leaves no memorial in the way,
   To ascertain that it has been.

14 The sovereign mercies of the LORD,
   Through everlasting age endure ;
   And children's children shall record
   His righteousness and goodness sure.

15 Who in his Covenant abide,
   Mind and perform his precepts just ;
   In heav'n for ever shall reside,
   Rais'd up in glory from the dust.

16 The LORD in heaven prepares his throne,
   His Kingdom ruleth over all :

His just dominion all must own,
Throughout the whole terrestrial ball,
And prostrate down before him fall,
The rich, the poor, the great, the small.

17 Ye Angels that excel in might,
And listen to his pow'rful word,
In fervent praise to him unite,
And in full concert, bless the LORD.

18 Bless him, all his attending Host,
Ye Ministers that do his will:
Through every land, in every coast,
All who his vast dominions fill!

19 My soul and all within me join,
In this blest harmony divine:
To fear his name, to love his word,
And ever celebrate the LORD.

Psalm CIV.

The transcendent glory and majesty of GOD, *displayed in the works of Creation and Providence, with devout aspirations.*

My soul the great JEHOVAH bless,
And his exalted name confess,
In humble and devout address.

Vested with majesty and might,
He reigns by his creative right,
In everlasting lustre bright.

With light as with a robe array'd,
The vast expansive heavens he made,
And like a curtain them outspread.

The fleeting wat'ry world he guides,
And there, as every where, resides:
The clouds which float in azure sky
A chariot to the LORD supply.

He walks on winds' impetuous wing
Gives life and breath to every thing.
Angels with energy inspires,
His ministers makes flaming fires.

The Earth he pois'd in empty air
To roll and turn for ages there.
Above he plac'd the swelling deep,
The waters o'er the hills did creep;
Driven by his awful reprimand
And voice of thunder from the land,
The mountains they ascend and flow
Descending to the vales below,
And pass to the determin'd space
Appointed to them for a place.
Thou to their rage a bound hast set,
O'er which, though they may foam and fret
With violence, they never can
O'erwhelm the world and ruin man.

The vales with liquid springs he fills,
Which run among adjoining hills:
Here quadrupeds of every name,
With asses wild, partake the stream.
The birds which neighbouring branches throng,
Express their joy in pleasant song.
From reservoirs which GOD has made
The mountains are with waters fed.

Thy works consummate and complete,
Proclaim thee, BLEST CREATOR ! *great !*
Thy creatures satisfy'd with food,
With gratitude pronounce THEE, *good !*

The ground in verdant grass array'd,
He pasture for the cattle made ;
And herbs in rich abundance grants
To satisfy all human wants.
The fertile earth by labour till'd,
A full return will always yield.
He cheers man's heart with grateful wine,
Gives oil to make his face to shine :

But no gift on our tables spread
Can equal that of strengthening bread.

The lofty trees which GOD has made
Afford us a delightful shade :
In Lebanon the Cedar's crest
Exceeds in majesty the rest:
The birds in safety there repose ;
The Stork her nest on fir-trees throws.
In hills the wild goat finds a place,
Rocks shelter well the Coney race.

For seasons GOD appoints the Moon,
And guides the setting of the Sun.
Darkness takes place at GOD's command,
And gloomy night involves the land.
The savage beasts who lay conceal'd
In forests wild, are now reveal'd :
The lions young, with frightful roar,
Now hunt their prey, their food explore ;
When Sun returns to cheer the day,
With eager speed they haste away,
And to their dens in silence creep,
And spend their time in rest or sleep.

A life so indolent and vain
May suit the savage race,—not men.
To labour Man goes forth abroad,
Performs the task assign'd by GOD :
Nor does from his exertion cease,
Till evening brings him rest and peace.

O LORD, omnipotent, and kind,
How manifold thy works, we find,
In wisdom thou hast all things made,
Thy riches through the earth are spread !

So is the great and spacious sea,
Where life in numerous forms we see,
Some large and frightful, others small,
Produced by thee, the LORD of all.

E

There ships perform their bold career,
To every coast and country steer.
Leviathan thou mak'st to roam,
And find in Ocean's depth,—a home.

These creatures both of land and sea
For food in season wait on thee :
What thy indulgent goodness grants,
They gather to relieve their wants ;
Thy open hand supplies their food,
Partaking, they are fill'd with good.
Dost thou withdraw thy smiling face,
For trouble they can find no ease ;
Thou tak'st away their fleeting breath,
And they return to dust by death.
The spirit which from thee proceeds
Creates and forms successive breeds :
Through earth renew'd fresh beauties shine,
All flowing from thy hand benign.

Through future ages as the past,
The glory of the LORD shall last :
With lustre still increasing spread ;
GOD *shall rejoice in all he made.**
Earth trembles at his awful look,
At his least touch the hills do smoke.

While life continues, I will sing
Unto the LORD, my gracious king ;
I'll praise him with my latest breath,
And trust his mercy even in death :
Sweet shall this meditation be ;
I will rejoice, O LORD in thee !

* *The* LORD *shall rejoice in all his works.*

This passage alone would almost convince me of the truth of that cheering benevolent doctrine,—the future, universal happiness of all mankind; and when taken in connection with other similar passages, its force becomes irresistible. How GOD can rejoice in misery and sin, I cannot conceive ! I think it is probable that *Thomson* had this noble sentiment of the Psalmist in view, when he composed that inimitable line,

——————————————————— "taste
" The joy of GOD, to see a happy world."

I do not believe, however, as some do, that there will be no future punishment at all ; but I believe, that all future punishment will cease when it has effected its proper object,—the Reformation of Offenders.

Let Sinners to conversion come,
Or in the earth no more find room :
Let wickedness expire and cease,
And be exchang'd with holiness.
My soul the LORD for ever bless,
All praise him and his grace confess.

Psalm cx.

Jesus the Messiah exalted, by the downfal of civil and ecclesiastical Tyranny, and the universal reception and establishment of the Gospel in its purity, in the latter days.

1 JEHOVAH, self existent LORD,
   Who rules in heaven, in earth and sea ;
By *David's* firm, prophetic word,
   Thus publish'd his supreme decree :
Which none can alter or repeal,
Confirm'd by an Almighty seal.

2 My *Son*, exalted from the pit,
   Now by my grace made *Lord* and *King*,
At my right hand in glory sit,
   Till ruin on thy foes I bring :
And cause them to thy power submit,
And prostrate fall before thy feet.

3 The LORD from *Zion* shall send forth,
   Thy rod of majesty and strength,
That rod shall rule th' astonish'd earth,
   Subduing enemies at length :
All opposition shall be vain,
To thy just, salutary reign.

4 A willing people shall appear,
   In thy great day of power and grace,
To hail thee, and still persevere
   In the blest paths of holiness :
Num'rous as dewy drops of morn,
Their youth thy age and church adorn.

5 The Lord hath sworn and will not break,
    A promise ratify'd in heaven;
In order of Melchizedek,
    A Priesthood I to thee have given:
Which never, never, shall decay,
But flourish and remain alway.

6 The Lord at thy right hand shall strike
    Opposing Kings in proud array;
Display his wrath and just dislike,
    In this renown'd eventful day
The heathen, he shall judge, restrain,
And fill each place with bodies slain.

7 The heads which now in grandeur shine,
    And rule great countries, he shall wound,
Shall baffle every vain design,
    And all their policy confound:
The brook divine shall cheer the road,
And lift his head to heaven and God.

Psalm cxxi.

Protection and Security only to be found in God.

1 Up to the hills I'll lift my eyes,
    From whence my hopes of safety spring;
The Lord, who made the earth and skies,
    Will help me and deliv'rance bring.

2 Thy feet shall still securely stand;
    He slumb'reth not who thee doth keep,
Who *Israel* keeps with mighty hand
    Shall neither slumber take nor sleep.

3 The Lord thy keeper is alway,
    On thy right hand he shall thee shade;
The Sun thee shall not smite by day,
    Nor Moon by night afflict thy head.

4 The LORD thy guardian shall abide,
   He shall preserve thy soul from ill ;
Thy going, coming, he shall guide,
   Protect thee now, and ever will.

—————

Psalm CXXV.

The stability and perseverance of the Godly ; the punishment of Apostacy.

1 Who trust in GOD, by him belov'd,
   As *Zion's* lofty mount shall be ;
The base of which shall not be mov'd,
   But last as long as earth and sea.

2 As mountains on all sides surround
   Jerusalem, of ancient fame ;
The LORD in mercy now is found
   About all those who own his Name,
   And will for ever bless the same.

3 The cruel and remorseless rod
   Of wicked men shall not abide,
To gall the Righteous, lest from GOD
   They should apostatize and slide.

4 O LORD, all gracious and kind ;—
   To those who choose the better part
Thy goodness shew ; be still inclin'd
   To favour the upright in heart.

5 But as for those who turn aside
   From Virtue, to their crooked way,
The LORD shall lead them forth, when try'd,
   With Sinners in the Judgment-day :
But peace to *Israel* shall be given
On earth, and still increas'd in heaven.

Psalm CXXVIII.

The blessings of the religious Man.

Blest is each one that fears the LORD,
Walks in his ways, and loves his word:

Thy toil and active industry
Shall food procure abundantly:
Contented, happy, thou shalt be,
In all it shall be well with thee.

Thy virtuous, kind and faithful spouse,
A fruitful vine, shall fill thy house:
Thy children dutiful be found,
Like olive plants, thy table round:
Behold, thus shall the Man be blest
Who fears the LORD, his joy, his rest.

The LORD from *Zion* shall thee bless,
And grant thy pious plans success:
Jerus'lem's good thou shalt behold,
In days of youth, and ev'n when old:
Thou shalt thy children's children see,
With peace on *Israel*, and thee.

Psalm CXXX.

Penitential mourning, joined with comfortable hope, and trust in divine mercy.

From depths of sin, and painful grief,
I cry to thee, LORD, for relief
My voice, O LORD, most gracious, hear,
To my entreaties lend an ear.

If thou, with unrelenting hand
Should'st mark transgressions, who shall stand?
But thine forgiveness is, O LORD,
That fear'd thou may'st be and ador'd.

I wait for God, with anxious heart,
His promises sweet hopes impart :
More earnestly for God I mourn
Than those that watch for cheerful morn ;
More anxiously than those, I say,
Who watch for the first dawn of day.

Let *Israel* in the Lord confide,
Mercy with him shall still reside :
Redemption free, and unconfin'd,
Is found with him for all mankind :
Israel, by grace, he shall redeem,
From all transgression, guilt and shame.

Psalm cxxxix.

The Omniscience and Omnipresence of God: *the admirable frame of Man: declarations of sincerity, and divine assistance implored.*

Thy piercing all discerning eye,
Hath search'd and known me, Lord *most high!*
My times of exercise and rest,
My acts, words, secrets of my breast :
Where'er I am, whate'er I do,
Stands open to thy perfect view :
My purposes to thee are clear
Before they to myself appear :
Before, behind, at sea, by land,
I feel and recognize thy hand :
Such knowledge all research transcends,
In wonder lost my labour ends.

Should I ascend the starry sky,
To the most distant planets fly ;
In *Herschel's* orb* fix my abode,
Ev'n there I find thee, O my God.

* Called in England the *Georgium Sidus*, in compliment to the late King of Great Britian : but on the continent of Europe, and in America, by the name of that great Astronomer who discovered it, as inserted above. It is a planet of vast size, and situated at an immense distance from the Sun.

Should I to the deep centre pierce
Of this terrestrial Universe ;
In gloomy caverns there reside,
This could not from thy presence hide.

If on the wings of morning light,
I take my bold, aspiring flight,
To penetrate the ocean wide,
And dwell where farthest flows the tide ;
Ev'n there thy hand shall guide my way,
Thy right hand hold me fast alway.

If my blind heart should dare to say,
Darkness shall screen me, if not day ;
The dun obscurity of night
Shall change to lustre, heav'nly bright.
For darkness veils not from thy sight,
But in thy view appears as light :
To thy perspicuous eye divine,
Both with an equal brightness shine.

From thee my reins and pow'rs all come,
Who form'd me in my mother's womb.
I'll praise thee for the skill display'd
Through all that frame thy goodness made ;
How marvellous thy works appear,
My mind well knows, and will declare.
The embryo mass unfinish'd lay,
Yet obvious was to thy survey ;
In parts extreme, divinely wrought,
With artifice beyond all thought :
My substance was to thee reveal'd,
While yet in secrecy conceal'd :
My complex members in thy book
Inscrib'd, from thence their fashion took ;
When none of them as yet appear'd,
In progress all by thee were rear'd.

O God how precious unto me
Are all thy thoughts of mercy free ;
The sum of all how great, how full,
To count them far exceeds my skill :
More num'rous than the grains of sand,
Found on the surface of the land.

The wicked thou shalt surely slay
O God :—depart from me, I say,
All who a savage pleasure find,
To shed the blood of human kind :
For wickedly they thee defame,
And thy foes falsely take thy name.
Do not I hate their ways, O Lord ?
Who hate thee and reject thy word :
Do I not for their conduct grieve ?
Do I not try to cure, relieve ?
As foes to thee, I hate their way,
But still for their conversion pray.

Search me, O God, and know my heart,
Try all my thoughts,—thy grace impart :
If any bitter root remain,
Be it extirpated and slain :
Let me be never led astray,
But tread the everlasting way.

Psalm CXLV.

The greatness of God ; *his benevolence and mercy, gratuitous and universal : the only foundation of hope and
trust.*

1 I'll praise thee, O my God, my King,
   And bless thy name for evermore :
Thy mercies daily comfort bring,
   And still remain in endless store.

2 Each day thy goodness grants to me,
   My gratitude shall still express ;
Nor shall this feeling cease to be,
   But through eternity increase.

3 The Lord, how wise ! how just ! how great !
   His greatness all research exceeds,
And each successive age, and state,
   Shall celebrate his mighty deeds.

F

4 Thy glorious honour, majesty,
  And wond'rous works in earth and heav'n
Shall still be kept in memory,
  And be my theme, while life is given.

5 Others shall add their names to mine,
  When I thy greatness shall declare,
And with abundant utt'rance join
  To sing thy goodness, justice, fair.

6 The Lord in gracious design,
  Exceeds whate'er we can entreat;
Compassions, far beyond our line,
  In him, in full assemblage, meet.

7 His goodness he to all displays,
  Who breathe the air or tread the ground,
His tender mercies' cheering rays,
  O'er all his matchless works are found.

8 Thy works consummate all shall praise
  Thee, Lord; thy Saints shall bless thy name,
Thy glorious kingdom, power and ways,
  Shall be their known and constant theme.

9 That so the heedless sons of men,
  May be to close attention driven,
To comprehend thy glorious plan,
  And own the majesty of heaven.

10 Thy kingdom, righteous and pure,
  Hath stood throughout all ages past,
And thy dominion shall endure
  While future generations last.

11 The Lord upholdeth all that fall,
  The bow'd-down, raiseth up to stand :
All creatures look to thee, and call,
  And find their portion from thy hand.

12 Thy hand unsparing, gracious, kind,
   To satisfy the pressing wants.
Of every living thing inclin'd;
   Their necessary portion grants.

13 The LORD in righteousness excels,
   In all his perfect plans it shines;
And holiness, which in him dwells,
   Pervades his works and his designs.

14 The LORD, who dwells in heav'n, *most high*,
   To all who worship him in truth
Is ever with his favour nigh;
   To feeble age and lively youth.

15 He will fulfil the just desire
   Of those that fear and love him still;
Will hear their cry and humble pray'r,
   And save them, if they do his will.

16 The LORD preserves with tender care,
   All those who love him and remain
In duty's path, and them will spare;
   But wickedness shall end in pain.

17 My mouth, with sacred zeal inspir'd,
   Shall speak the praises of the LORD;
And let all flesh, with rapture fir'd,
   His holy name and grace record,
   And ever, ever, bless the LORD,
   With cheerful voice, and full accord. }

CHRISTMAS HYMNS.

No. i.

AN IMPROMPTU,

On the birth of Jesus Christ, the Son of God.—Composed on Christmas eve ; Philadelphia, 24th of December, 1812.

While others sing the sad exploits of war,
The crimson'd deck, and " garments roll'd in blood,"
The heroes whose exertions have subdu'd
Strong bands of proud and pow'rful enemies,
On their own element—the sea itself!
With signal naval glory and renown ; *
I sing the mild and the pacific birth,
Of Jesus, friend of frail humanity,
By whose kind aid and gracious relief,
Man was restor'd to life—immortal life,
And liberty more true than any other,
The glorious freedom of the sons of God ;
Deliverance from vice and all the passions,
Which mangle and disfigure human nature,
And fill the world with tumult and confusion,
With death, destruction, and a train of evils
Grievous beyond all measure and expression.

Angels from heav'n with joy announc'd the birth
Of this illustrious hero, and pronounc'd
In strains seraphic and melodious,
" Glory to God, our Father, in the highest,
" May peace, the best of blessings, be on earth,
" And great good will to all the human race."†

May what these angels sung be realiz'd,
And war with all its horrors cease for ever.

An Old Scotsman,

And a real friend to the U. States of America,
and the present administration.

* Captains Hull, Jones and Decatur, and the brave officers and seamen under their command.

† Luke ii. 8 to 14.

CHRISTMAS DAY, 1814.

NO. II.

Blest was the day, and glorious was the hour,
When GOD in mercy great did richly pour
His choicest blessings, by the joyful birth
Of JESUS, Saviour of Heav'n and Earth.*
But let *Earth* blush, so meanly to afford,
Accommodation for its gracious Lord!
Born in a Stable, in a manger held,
The glorious infant Saviour was beheld,
By Eastern Sages, upright men and true,
Who came, led by a Star, with joy to view,
His sacred person, and forthwith proclaim'd
Him *King of Jews*, and justly Sovereign nam'd.
Angels of God, array'd in Heav'nly light,
Declar'd the blissful tidings in the night,
To humble Shepherds on the rural plain,
With acclamation great and joyful strain.
To you, in David's city, there is born,
A Saviour, Christ the Lord, who shall adorn
The Sons of Men, with truth and Heav'nly grace,
The greatest treasures of the human race.
Glory to God, the spacious concave rung,
Peace be on earth, good will to men, they sung,
Come let us join the sweet celestial Song,
And in loud notes the sacred strains prolong:
Glory to God, our Heav'nly Father say,
Peace be on Earth, good will, and endless day. †

AN AMERICAN CITIZEN.

* Col. 1. 16.&c.   "For by him were all things created (or renewed) that are in Heaven, and that are in Earth, &c."
† *Day*, in scripture, is metaphorically used to denote joy, light, happiness, piety, tranquility, &c. in opposition to *night*, the emblem of darkness, ignorance, misery and vice.

NO. III.

CHRISTMAS DAY. 1815.

1 To great JEHOVAH's name be praise,
   Who on this sacred day,
   From *David's seed* a *branch* did raise*
   To rule the Church alway.

* Isaiah xi 1 to 9. Jeremiah xxiii. 5, 6—Acts xiii. 22, 23—2 Tim. ii. 3—Rev. xxii. 16.

2 Below the usual degree
    Of mortals here on earth,
  The light of heav'n he first did see,
    And started into birth.

3 The glorious Saviour was rear'd
    Like any other child,
  No splendid pomp in him appear'd,
    But all was plain and mild.

4 Though men in general knew him not,
    And scorn'd his humble state,
  Angels on high declare his *lot*,†
    And celebrate his fate.

5 Ordain'd of God to bless each land
    With truth and righteousness,
  His kingdom shall for ever stand
    In equity and peace.‡

† Luke ii. 11 to 14.
‡ Having composed and published two pieces for Christmas day before the present, in which I have enlarged on the circumstances which attended our ever honoured Saviour's birth, I have to avoid repetition, touched upon these circumstances very briefly in the foregoing piece.

CHRISTMAS DAY, 1816.

No. IV.

1 Delightful day, which first beheld
    The infant Saviour's face ;
  For ages promis'd but withheld,
    Till the appointed space.

2 No childish sport, in early youth
    His serious mind possess'd ;
  Wisdom, benignity and truth,
    Resided in his breast.

3 The Doctors in the Temple saw,
    With admiration fill'd,
  A child instructed in the Law,
    A boy in knowledge skill'd.

4 His mind, maturing as he grew,
    Fresh graces still display'd,
  Favour from God, his virtue drew,
    And men attention paid.

5 When thirty years had fill'd their rounds,
    To Jordan's flood he came,
And ent'ring in the wat'ry bounds,
    John dip'd him in the stream.

6 From op'ning Heav'n now fill'd his eye,
    A beam of sacred light,
The energy of GOD *Most High*,
    Descending on him, bright.

7 A voice was heard, in solemn tone,
    And words express and clear :
" This is my well-beloved Son,
    " Approv'd, and ever dear."

8 This Heav'nly voice, let all inspire ;
    Let all with firm accord,
Embrace with joy and warm desire,
    Th' *anointed* of the LORD.

9 While Sun and Moon in Heav'n do roll,
    Shall stand his righteous cause,
And nations plac'd from pole to pole,
    Shall hail him with applause.

CHRISTMAS DAY, 1817.

No. v.

Glory to God in the highest, and on Earth peace, good will
towards men !

" SING Heav'nly Muse" the Saviour's birth,
The day of jubilee to earth ;
Reversing guilty Adam's fall,
Restoring life and peace to all,
Announcing love divine to men,
In accents of Angelic strain ;
Proclaiming universal grace,
Without reserve of time or place.

The blessings promis'd why delay'd ?
Why ling'ring in the Covenant made ?
Why are destruction's flags unfurl'd,
And horrid wars defile the world ?
Tyrants assume the pow'r divine,
And cause men worship at their shrine ?

Presumptuous words ! to God alone,
Are his wise plans and counsels known :
With reverence read the sacred page,
Let prophecy your mind engage ;
There you will see as in a glass,
The scenes of pride and empire pass.
Destruction fall on lawless pow'r,
The short-liv'd triumph of an hour ;
The king dethron'd and servile priest,
And all who venerate the Beast
To desolation brought, and driven
From every country under Heaven !

Meantime let all the Sons of Grace,
Possess their minds in love and peace ;
Relieve each others' wants and shew
A Heav'nly temper here below.

Columbia's land, " the mercy-seat,"
Be open as a safe retreat
To shield the wretched, and afford
A rest to all who love the LORD.

CHRISTMAS DAY, 1818.

No. VI.

Unto us a Child is born : unto us a Son is given, &c.
—Grace and Truth came by Jesus Christ.

1 To us, this day, a Child is born :
    To us, a promis'd Son is given,
  Whose lustre shall the earth adorn,
    And fill the vast expanse of heaven.

2 A Messenger of great Design ;
    His counsels truth and grace display ;
  Father of future age divine ;
    The Prince of Peace, mild as the day.

3 His sway pacific shall prevail,
    Through circling ages safe remain,
  On David's throne and kingdom still,
    He Right and Justice shall maintain.

4 What pow'r benignant shall reveal,
    This King sublime on all our coasts ?
  JEHOVAH's favour, love and *zeal*,
    The GOD of Grace, and heavenly hosts.

CHRISTMAS DAY, 1819.

No. VII.

Ubi amatur, non laboratur ;
Et si laboratur, Labor amatur.

THAT IS,

" Where Love is, there is no labour ; and if there be labour,
" the labour is loved."—*Augustine.*

O for a song of sacred mirth,
To celebrate the Saviour's birth ;
Who at his heavenly Father's call,
Brought life and liberty to all.

Glory to God, the LORD *Most High,*
Who fram'd the earth, and starry sky,
Whose wisdom form'd the gracious plan,
To renovate degenerate man ;
And *Jesus* sent our race to bless,
Richly adorn'd with truth and grace ;—
To burst the barriers of the grave,
Omnipotent to heal and save.

Let *Homer* from Parnassus' mount,
His Grecian heroes' acts recount,
Exhibit fierce Achilles' rage,
Style him the champion of the age.

Let *Virgil* in majestic verse,
Renown'd Æneas' deeds rehearse.

Let *Horace* tune the Pagan lyre,
Enraptur'd with poetic fire,
And hail Augustus Cæsar's name,
With others of distinguish'd fame.

My task be, to my latest breath,
To sing the MAN *of Nazareth ;*
Who still the paths of virtue trod,
Gentle, humane, *approv'd of God.*

CHRISTMAS DAY. 1820.

No. VIII.

1 When Abraham with prophetic eye,
The future Saviour did descry,
The pleasing prospect did impart
The purest joy to his fond heart.

G

2 In him he saw all nations blest,
   Grace publish'd, sacred truth confest ;
   The idol-temples overthrown,
   Jehovah own'd as GOD alone.

3 David in grand poetic strain
   Foretold the great Messiah's reign ;
   Isaiah hail'd him *Prince of Peace*,
   By whose controul all wars should cease.

4 Did the delightful foretaste charm
   These Saints, their breasts with rapture warm :
   Shall our cold hearts remain unmov'd,
   Nor love the *Man*, who all men lov'd ?

5 Hail ! Son of David, Abra'm, God,
   Who seal'd his doctrine with his blood !
   Rejoice O ! Heavens, be glad O ! Earth,
   At this exalted Saviour's Birth !

ODE FOR THE NEW YEAR, 1815.

A WISH FOR PEACE.

Pax est optima rerum.

Fourteen is finished, *fifteen* now comes on,
What may take place, to mortals is unknown :
But known to God, to whose imperial sway,
All things in Heav'n and Earth of right obey.
God grant the op'ning year, before it cease,
May bring about *the best of blessings*, PEACE.
May sheath the bloody sword the soldier's pain,
And give tranquility to earth and main :
May Commerce flourish, Manufactures grow,
And Agriculture bless the earth below.
May justice, truth and equity preside,
And wisdom, virtue, all our counsels guide,
Religion flourish, and in all hearts reign,
And vice be bound with adamantine chain.

Verses for GOOD FRIDAY, *April* 12, 1816.

On *Friday*, strange and wonderful to tell !
JESUS, the wise, the just, the *Saviour* fell,
A sacrifice to Jewish hate and pride,
Which prompted them with malice to deride
His suff'rings sad and agonizing pain,
In speeches ludicrous and impious strain.

The Priests and Rulers to reflection blind,
Harden'd in guilt and reprobate in mind,
Vainly imagin'd they had overcome
His pow'r divine, and fix'd his lasting doom.

But GOD whose plans are matchless and sublime,
Unchang'd by events, unconfin'd by time,
From JESUS' death made endless blessings flow
To all the human family below :
Forgiveness free to all the penitent,
Attested by his blood in covenant ;
A Pattern great of firmness to maintain
The cause of GOD before the face of men,
And to give up our lives and all we have
When duty calls, a victim to the grave ;
Secure that all we lose shall be restor'd
In life eternal, by our gracious LORD.*

A SALUTE TO PHILADELPHIA,

After an absence of near two months.

Hail Philadelphia, happy seat,
Where beauty, health, convenience, meet !
Apart from thee my health declin'd,
Feeble in body and in mind.
With joy I visit thy domain,
And see a thousand graces reign.

Here, Schuylkill rolls its gentle waves,
There, Delaware its billows heaves :
Thy streets in even angles end ;
No crooked turn, distorted bend.
How many stately structures rise,
To greet the Sovereign of the skies :.
No privilege of sect is found,
All stand on fair and equal ground.
Thy Stores of neat and ample size,
Are full of useful merchandize ;
Provisions of all kinds abound,
And ever in thy markets found.
Science and taste, mechanic arts,
Here flourish, and maintain their parts.
Thy wharves a numerous fleet display,
With hardy seamen fresh and gay.

* For a full relation of the particulars of our Saviour's Crucifixion, see a Poem, entitled, *Jesus the Messiah*, &c. Canto V.

Go on, and prosper, still increase,
Under the fostering hand of peace ;
Look up to Heaven, implore its aid,
And trust in God, who all things made.

Philadelphia, December 13, 1819.

ELEGY

On the the late Benjamin Smith Barton, M. D. Professor
of the Theory and Practice of Medicine, and of Natural
History, and Botany, in the University of Pennsylvania.

Nec prosunt Domino, quæ prosunt omnibus artes !

Ovid.

" No longer his all healing art avails ;
" But every remedy its Master fails !"

1 Death has arrested Barton, now no more,
     In full career of life's meridian stage ;
No more his penetration shall explore
     Arts salutary both to youth and age.

2 The hand which oft administer'd relief
     To patients sinking in disease and pain,
Wasted with sickness and worn out with grief,
     Lies stiff and torpid in the dreary plain.

3 The brain in which ideas clear and just,
     In brisk and lively currents quickly rose,
Disorganiz'd and broken in the dust,
     Can nothing now exhibit or disclose.

4 The tongue which manna dropt and sweetness led
     To sooth the languid sufferer's distress,
Lock'd up and still among the silent dead,
     The tender feelings can no more express.

5 Long did he struggle to retrieve his health,
     Try'd every art that medicine can yield,
But life can not be bought by skill or wealth,
     By learning's light or heroes in the field.

6 When Am'ric's land no succour could afford,
     To foreign climes he hasten'd to repair
His wasting strength, and to confirm the cord
     Of brittle life, by change of scene and air.

7 But all in vain, *France* could no safety bring,
   Nor *Britain* high in medical renown,
  Both lands he left, return'd on naval wing
   To his blest native land and pleasant town.

8 He linger'd out the last remains of day,
   In Freedom's mansion and in friendly arms,
  Retain'd his faculties without decay,
   And bid adieu to earth and mortal charms.

9 Now, change the scene, anticipate the hour,
   When Death shall yield his spoils and Grave its prey,
  By the resistless force and conqu'ring pow'r
   Of CHRIST descending in a heav'nly ray.

10 Then *Barton* shall appear, I humbly trust,
   In form superior to his mortal dress,
  And rise triumphant from the crumbling dust
   To spend eternal age in perfect bliss.

Philadelphia, Thursday evening,
December 21st, 1815.

TO THE MEMORY OF THE LATE

Mrs. MELLISH.

Blessed are the dead who die in the LORD,—*that they may rest*
from their labours; and their works do follow them.—Rev.
xiv. 13.

   Farewell the wife, the mother and the friend!
A sweet domestic comfort at an end:
Thy mind was gentle, candid, calm, sincere,
True to thy husband, to thy children dear.
A tedious state of pain, for some time past,
Thou didst support with patience to the last:
A future day will bring, I fully trust,
A recompense to thee and all the *Just.*

Philadelphia, Tuesday, Feb. 4th, 1817.

To THE MEMORY OF THOMAS M‘KEAN,

Late Governor of Pennsylvania, this day interred.

An honest man's the noblest work of GOD!

                     POPE.

   M‘KEAN no more! the wise, the firm, the just,
Committed for a time to rest in dust:

His name shall live in Pennsylvania's State,
Be celebrated to a period late;
While Independence glows in every heart,
And Right, and Liberty their joys impart.*

* The late Mr. M'Kean, with many other Patriotic Delegates subscribed the Declaration of Independence, the Articles of Confederation, &c. and the Constitution of Pennsylvania. He came forward in his old age, at a dangerous crisis, in the late war, in support of his country, and for the defence of Philadelphia.

Philadelphia, June 26th, 1817.

———————

TO THE MEMORY OF

THOMAS FYSHE PALMER,

" Clergyman, sometime residing in Dundee, and commonly " designed Unitarian Minister,"* a native of Bedfordshire, in England, who died at Guam, an island, in the South Sea, on his return from Botany Bay, in the year 1802.

> *There sleeps the brave, now gone to rest,*
> *With every Patriot's wishes blest!*

Palmer! thou Christian Hero, friend of Man,
Whose life was duly form'd on Virtue's plan ;
The God of nature did to thee impart,
A firm, undaunted, yet a feeling heart ;
Soldier of Christ, who zealously profess'd,
The faith of JESUS, openly confess'd.
A system salutary, clear and true,
Founded on Reason and on Scripture too.
Where these two perfect principles unite,
Truth then shines forth with beams divinely bright.
Attracts the candid part of human kind,
And captivates the fair, discerning mind.

In England's church, born, bred, instructed, plac'd.
He might with Fortune's smiles and gifts been grac'd,
But these rejected were, and thrown away,
Yielded to Conscience call and rightful sway.
   A period equal to the siege of Troy,
In Caledonia's land he did employ,
Exerting strenuous labour, faithful care,
To storm the citadel of error there,

* So Mr. Palmer is styled in his indictment, and in the verdict of the Jury who condemned him. See the trial of the Rev. Thomas Fyshe Palmer, &c. taken in court by Mr. Ramsey, an eminent short-hand writer from London, and published by W. Skirving.

Without the hope or prospect of reward,
To sweeten mental toil, contention hard ;
All he desired, expected, was to gain
Converts to Christian truth, a numerous train.
In this humane and estimable plan,
Some success did attend this active man.

Who lo! in his tenth year of labour great,
The people's minds were turn'd t' affairs of State ;
Parties were form'd, some for reform exclaim'd,
The Friends of Government oppos'd, defam'd.
My generous, open, unsuspecting friend,
His help gratuitous did nobly lend
To those who did espouse the people's cause,
The side of liberty and equal laws :
For this was try'd, condemn'd, and sent away,
In Exile for seven years to Botan' Bay.
This term expir'd, he hastened to return,
Died by the way, and rested in his urn.

To mortal views this Providence seems strange,
If forward with the eyes of faith we range,—
The Judge Supreme of this great universe
Will every partial, cruel deed reverse,
To suffering Virtue will award a crown,
And Martyrs compensate with just renown.

Philadelphia, Friday evening, June 15th, 1821.

TO THE MEMORY OF THE LATE

MRS. AGNES CHRISTIE,

Who died on Friday, the 26th of January, 1821, in the 73d
year of her age.

JESUS WEPT.

———— " *When such friends part,*
" *'Tis the Survivor dies.*"

" Yes, while remembrance hold its seat,
" *This breast* shall feel regret ;
" The wounded heart may cease to beat,
" But never can forget."

Friend of my youth, and partner of my life,
My much lamented, venerated Wife!

Sweet modesty and unaffected grace,
Brightened thy features and adorn'd thy face :
The sympathetic feelings filled thy breast,
Good will to all, pity to the distrest ;
No base, malignant passions fir'd thy mind,
To purity and innocence consign'd.
Train'd in the paths of virtue from thy youth,
With veneration for religious truth,
The precious fruits of piety appear'd
In early age, and thy blest bosom cheer'd,
Charm'd all thy friends, and with instructive force
Made others imitate thy virtuous course.

Happy for me, that I was quickly moved
To see thy merit, and thy plans approv'd ;
That I, of others, did succeed alone,
To make such worth and excellence my own.

When first conjoin'd, I found her closely bound
In *Orthodoxy's* chain and doctrines *sound*.
With tenderness and skill I then began
To intimate a pure and liberal plan :
To sacred Scripture made a strong appeal,
With prudence join'd with a becoming zeal.
At first, indeed, with very small success,
But Heav'n at last was pleas'd the work to bless,
All prejudice and error did give way
Quite overcome by Truth's superior ray ;
Unclouded views broke in and heavenly light,
And she shone forth, an UNITARIAN BRIGHT :
Fix'd, rivetted, unshaken she remain'd,
And sacred truth with fortitude maintain'd.
To friends and relatives though ever kind,
She followed still the dictates of her mind :
Where Conscience pointed she pursued the road,
Alone, *Christ master, Father none, but God!*
In SCOTLAND, more than thirty years, ago,
For six long miles unwearied she would go
To join in worship pure, and calmly hear,
The Truth maintain'd by reasons strong and clear.

When in the course of Providence she came,
To this *free land*, of justly *glorious name*,
No greater joy occurred on other ground,
Than in the UNITARIAN CHURCH she found.
Even to the latest period of her life.
She shewed the Parent kind ; the faithful Wife ;

And with increas'd activity pursu'd
A course of usefulness and doing good.
Though at the time of death depriv'd of speech,
Her patience, gentleness, did more than preach.
In calmness she gave up her mortal breath,
And sweetly sunk in the cold arms of death.

Dearest of Women, now I bid farewell,
Till we shall meet again where pleasures dwell
Pure and untainted, subject to no change,
But lasting through eternity's wide range,
Increasing and improving in full store,
And never to be separated more!
Still I will love thee to my latest breath,
And be a constant *Widower*, till Death!
Philadelphia, Saturday, January 27th, 1821.

---

*A wise and useful Old Age contrasted with the too frequent
pursuits of Youth.*

" That the aged men be sober, (or vigilant) grave, temperate,
sound in faith, in charity, in patience."   *Titus* ii. 2.
   Omnium ætatum certus est terminus : senectutis autem nul-
lus certus est terminus : recteque in ea vivitur, quoad munus
officii exsequi et tueri possis, et tamen mortem contemnere
ex quo fit, ut animosior etiam senectus sit quam adolescentia
et fortior.

Old Age I sing, with long Experience join'd,
Source of good sense, and rectitude of mind ;
If wisdom in the compact join its part,
Inform the head and regulate the heart.
In Youth too oft the passions rove at large ;
Reason is weak and heedless of its charge :
Passion assumes the reins and rushes on
Like *Phaeton* in the chariot of the sun.
On this side Pleasure spreads her Syren charms,
Corrupts the mind and fortitude disarms :
On that, Ambition fires the youthful soul,
Impetuous, fierce, forbidding all controul,
Panting for fame, distinction, wealth or pow'r,
Vain pageantry and creatures of an hour.

How often do the votaries of fame
Perish obscurely, fall without a name ;
Or if some portion of renown they gain,
How dear the price, what endless toil and pain !
                    H

When Wealth, a darling object, is pursu'd,
And sought by every method bad and good,
If not attain'd the character is lost,
Contempt succeeds and merited distrust.
If *Mammon* smiles, and heaps on heaps are roll'd,
What dignity can rise from yellow gold?
If Virtue, precious Virtue, stand apart
And neither fill the head, nor warm the heart:
Fools may admire, and sycophants may paint,
But brave and honest minds refuse assent.

When now the term of giddy youth is past,
And cool reflecting *age* succeeds at last,
With sad regret and anguish we survey
Time infamously spent or thrown away.
Happy the man who can look back on time
Enjoy'd in innocence, unstain'd with crime.
But happy next, who with repenting heart,
Grieves for the past and takes the better part,
Corrects his faults and regulates his ways,
And spends in virtuous deeds his latter days.
How precious is *Old Age* when thus employ'd,
Each vicious tendency curb'd or destroy'd:
The mind awake to Reason, every sense
Inspir'd with virtue and benevolence.
A bright example on this earthly stage
To form the manners of the rising age,
Join'd with instructive lessons, fit to move
The youthful mind, when seconded by love.

Devotion too must fully bear its part,
To cheer the mind and sanctify the heart,
Without this antidote and cordial charm,
Age must be languid, death create alarm.
Devotion points to heav'n, dispels the gloom
Of sinking nature, ready for the tomb,
With joy and hope we view the promis'd land,
And leave the world resign'd at GOD's command.

Philadelphia, Sunday evening, January 28th, 1816.

(159)

ADDENDA.

Mr. Palmer and Mrs. Christie were *lovely in their lives;* but in their deaths, they were very much *divided.* The former died in a strange and distant land, without an attendant that he could unbosom himself to, except his friend Mr. Ellis, whom he had adopted as his son. The latter, though deprived of the faculty of speech, was in possession of her senses, and expired in the presence of her husband, who endeavoured to catch her last breath. Her other affectionate friends (for obvious reasons,) had retired some hours before her death.

Mrs. Christie expressed, at different times, much esteem for the characters and labours of the two Ministers, who have discharged their duty with such exemplary fidelity in the *first* Church of Unitarian Christians in this city; and I have a real pleasure in exhibiting her sentiments before the public.

In a Note annexed to the Preface of *Dissertations on the Unity of God, &c.,* I expressed myself to this effect. " Mr. " Palmer (after he was settled in Scotland) made one excur- " sion into England, and preached powerfully at Newcastle, " and other places. It should have been *written* " two ex- " cursions."

Philadelphia, July 7th, 1821.   W. C.

FINIS.

www.ingramcontent.com/pod-product-compliance
Lightning Source LLC
Chambersburg PA
CBHW022035080426
42733CB00007B/842